CREATIVE MOVEMENT
for the DEVELOPING CHILD

A NURSERY SCHOOL HANDBOOK FOR NON-MUSICIANS

REVISED EDITION

CLARE CHERRY

Director
Congregation Emanu El Nursery School
San Bernardino, California

FEARON PITMAN PUBLISHERS, INC.

Belmont, California

To Dani, A Developing Child.

ISBN-0-8224-1660-3

Library of Congress Catalog Card Number: 79-125140

Printed in the United States of America

Foreword

Growth and development of the child from infancy through adolescence has been a subject of study for many years. Analytical observations have shown that the normal child will perform in a fairly consistent way, and that it is possible to predict what he will do at any given stage of development. Within this pattern, however, there are variables due to individual differences and the demands of a particular culture. It is mostly in the pre-school years that the mold is set for future physical, perceptual, and emotional responses.

In normal growth and development, the child goes through many phases of change. At birth, he has basic reflexes and preservation-of-life instincts. These are automatic and at a low level of brain function since high level brain structures are not fully developed at birth. As he grows, he is capable of learning at successively higher levels.

From basic reflex patterns, he begins to develop from head-to-toe and from in-to-out. The baby starts to hold his head up and tries to grasp for things off to the side if they are put near his hand. He uses his fingers and his palms for holding. Then he learns to bring his hands to midline so that he can grasp hold of and look at objects from the front. Through various progressive stages, he begins to use the thumb and index finger to pick up things. During these early months of development, the child first uses his mouth for touching and feeling, gradually replacing this with the use of his hands as he grows. This very important process of touching and feeling precedes visual recognition or understanding of seen objects. As these objects are seen and felt, they take on meaning. This is cognitive learning. Since touch is the only physical contact we have with things, it is probably the most important sense we have. Millions of impulses go to the brain daily from oral, hand, and body feeling. The more of these sensory impulses the child experiences, the more sensitive the impressions become and the quicker skills are developed.

By the time a child is between six and eight months of age, he tries to get up on his hands and knees, first rocking back and forth, and then propelling himself forward by creeping. This is often preceded by rolling, scooting or crawling on the abdomen, using the hands and arms to pull and the legs to push.

These movements cannot be overstressed in normal growth as the experiences of horizontal bilateral movement seem to be important in the development of other mental functions such as speech and vision.

During these first six or eight months, the child is also learning to use his eyes in a meaningful way and to coordinate them with what the rest of his body is doing. At birth, each eye functions independently, and the eyes cannot focus on an object; but as the child grows and develops, they begin to work together as a unit. This is coordinated with hand movements, both as the child creeps or crawls, and as he picks up things that are desired.

There are two separate, but important factors in vision. One is the eyeball and the muscles controlling its movement. The other is what is called perception. Through the optic nerve, a signal is sent to the brain where objects that are seen take on meaning. Perception requires thought and reasoning; seeing does not. The same relationship is true between listening and hearing; listening is perception and hearing is not. It is through meaningful listening and the accompanying development of auditory perception that the child learns to speak and relate to the spoken word.

It is highly important that visual and auditory perception skills be developed to a high degree as they affect a person's physical relationship in space such as position and balance. Through the balance mechanism in the inner ear, we know when we are right side up, and messages from the brain are sent to various parts of the body to compensate for abnormal postural conditions. Likewise, brain messages are sent to the eye muscles to make visual corrections.

In essence, the principal objective of *Creative Movement for the Developing Child* is to develop an acute sensory perception during various stages of the child's growth in order to increase skills in areas of need. The human organism is constantly searching for something to which it can react. Interest is the force behind this constant search for a stimulus. By using the interests of the young child in motivating goal-directed action, we can help him to make maximum use of his capabilities.

DAVID W. GREENE
Child Development Consultant

Preface

Working in the field of early childhood is challenging and exciting because of the creativity which all children possess. The challenge is in the appreciation which the child expresses while he is yet young enough to respond freely without the inhibitions of societal pressures. The excitement is in the generosity with which a child gives of himself and to which sensitive adults respond.

This book is the outgrowth of that inspiration which I derived from the many children I have known at Congregation Emanu El Nursery in San Bernardino, California, and at other schools.

The activities presented in *Creative Movement for the Developing Child* are not sacred. Adapt, change, and experiment with the materials and suggestions offered in this book. Occasionally, slight changes in wording, rhyme scheme, or music have been made deliberately to take care of special needs. This is part of the philosophy of the program. Above all—have fun!

My personal thanks and gratitude are due to the following who have contributed so generously to *Creative Movement for the Developing Child*: Congregation Emanu El for giving me the freedom to pursue an experimental course in the development of a nursery school program as a service to the community; Rabbi Norman Feldheym, Cantor Robert Miller, and Dr. Martha Frank who guided my creative impulses into meaningful pursuits; Rabbi Hillel Cohn and Betty Zelman for their encouragement and advice; and Halliette Stubbs and Bettye Kovitz for their assistance in the development of the materials. My thanks are also due Alyce Smothers, Janet Peters, and Lael Cohen for trying out the ideas in the classroom; to Stephanie Viero, for her musical advice; and to Rae Magid, Edith Stelzer, Lillian West, Sharyla Gold, Edith Goldberg and the members of my own family for their practical assistance and for their moral support.

CLARE CHERRY

Contents

1 Creativity Begins with the Room Environment

The nursery school, like any other educational institution, is a place for learning. It provides a meaningful curriculum which builds important foundations for future reading skills and other academic pursuits. It provides appropriate play experiences which contribute to the overall growth and development of the child. Not only does he learn behavioral patterns that will assist him in adjusting to a highly complex social order; he learns how to develop and use his natural creative abilities that are so essential to living in a world that is becoming more and more mechanized.

Since nursery school children become involved in a multiplicity of activities, the stage must be set for the aesthetic awareness which children intuitively have. Until the child is approximately 2½ or 3 years of age, shape is a stronger factor to him than color. Between the ages of three and five, however, color becomes a dominant influence; therefore, color schemes in the classrooms should be selected with great care for a harmonious effect.

The creative environment must not only look attractive. It must be orderly and convenient so that the child is physically comfortable and secure in the knowledge that he knows where to find things. It should allow both for group and individual activities, with areas for quiet, restful pursuits and areas for creative activities of all kinds. Since most nursery classes use multiple-purpose rooms, they should be so arranged as to allow for maximum flexibility .

Consideration must be given to the ease with which a room can be kept in order so that the child can be taught to assume certain responsibilities in keeping play areas neat, clean, and attractive. Items used by the child must be returned to their proper place before another item is taken out or another type of activity pursued. The child can be inspired to do his part in helping to keep order if materials are presented in neat, colorful containers, and if storage areas and shelves for toys are arranged for maximum utility and attractiveness.

Available wall space for displaying pictures and illustrations should be considered in working out the decor of the rooms. This does not mean that the teacher should clutter the walls with meaningless displays or useless objects. A teacher who has all wall space covered has fallen victim to the mistaken idea that children need to be entertained all the time. A few simple illustrations placed at the child's eye level free him to use his imagination and to think creatively.

As needs arise, displays and room arrangements are changed from time to time; however, the entire room decor is never changed all at once. Enough items should be left in the same places at any one time to create a feeling of familiarity; yet enough things should be changed to stimulate a constant flow of new ideas. As much as possible, the child should be given an opportunity to help in planning the displays and arranging the various play areas.

Adult-oriented displays to impress parents and to satisfy teacher's ego. Although attractive, this room shows work obviously finished by the teacher to bring it closer to adult standards. Much of it is too high.

Child-oriented displays to please a child. No adult work on children's work. Most things are low enough for a child to touch, study and enjoy.

2 A Day at School

As each child arrives on a typical school day, he is greeted by the director, supervisor, or head teacher. He is then checked for general health appearance and possible symptoms of communicable disease. After these preliminaries, he is taken or sent to his classroom where he is further welcomed by his own teacher who has already spent half-an-hour or more readying her materials for the day's activities.

To the 2½ or 3 year old, nursery school seems like a long way from home. The child is greeted with close affection, perhaps even a hug, by his reassuring teacher. This warmth of greeting and sincerity of feeling establish a rapport with the child which may be reflected in his attitude about school from that point on.

One by one, each child finds his way to an activity. In the doll corner, two children become deeply engrossed in housekeeping. One sits on the floor, takes dishes from the shelf, places them all about her, and closely examines each piece over and over. Suddenly she arises, picks up the dishes, and carefully puts them on the small table beside her. The other child is busy with the dolls. She picks them up and places them in chairs around the table. Then she takes them out of the chairs, piles them into the doll bed, and bends down to cover them up. She changes her mind, takes them out of the bed, and places them in the doll buggy. Neither child is quiet for an instant.

Another child joins the group. He reaches for some pans and starts to "cook" at the stove. After a time, tiring of that activity, he gets down on the floor, crawls under the table to the other side of the housekeeping area, and runs across the room to get a large plastic truck out of a cupboard. He soon leaves the truck, and runs over to a table where the teacher has set out some percussion instruments. He decides on a maraca and, as he shakes it vigorously back and forth, the instrument rattles. Other children join him, and they experiment in handling some of the other instruments.

Later in the year, the teacher will help them in the use of the instruments; but this will be only after they have participated in many body movements and have developed sufficient motor ability. Now the teacher observes for awhile. Then she picks up a tambourine and, while shaking it quietly, she sings, "Time to put the toys a-way. Time to put the toys a-way." Now the children go on to other activities.

Similar activities are going on in rooms for 3½ to 4 year olds and four and five year olds.

In the middle group, children are building with blocks, working puzzles at a table or on the floor, cutting and pasting bits of colored paper, and generally going about their own business.

A child has brought his four-week-old pet rabbit to school in a cage. Several children are on their knees watching the rabbit as it hops all around its cage. As they watch in fascination, they begin to discuss how it hops and jumps, because these are the kinds of things their teacher has already taught them to observe and to think about. Suddenly one child begins hopping on her knees, kicking up her legs as she supports herself with her hands. "I'm a rab-bit. I'm a rab-bit," she says. The alert teacher takes a tambourine from a shelf and starts to shake it to the rhythm of the child's movements as she chants "Hip-pi-ty hop, hip-pi-ty hop, I'm going to get a car-rot top." Soon the entire group is hopping and laughing and jumping to the magic of the moment. The incident is not enlarged upon as it is time to go outdoors. But it will be referred to time and again during rhythmic activity sessions. Each child now busily puts away the things he had been playing with prior to the spontaneous rhythmic movement session and, with the teacher's help, all is soon in order. The group follows the teacher into the hall to put on coats and sweaters as she sings "Soft-ly on our tip-py toes, to the hall we go."

In the older class, the children are busier and noisier. The feeling is one of socialization, excitement and accomplishment. There is much sharing and cooperation as buildings are being constructed, blocks are being arranged, and dress-up clothes are being chosen. In one area of the room, some children are painting on large sheets of paper attached to painting boards that have been placed on blocks to raise them six to eight inches off the floor. This activity requires the children to be on the knees; and it involves much reaching and stretching to exchange cans of paint, to reach the far corners of the paper, and to satisfy the feeling for movement.

Across the room, the teacher is demonstrating the action of a pair of unusually heavy magnets. Each child takes a turn in feeling the attraction of the magnets to each other. They also discover that when the poles are reversed, they repel rather than attract. One ingenious child suggests making up a magnet game. The children choose partners, join hands, and experiment in finding out whether they need to push or to pull to be "magnets." Soon many are moving rhythmically as the teacher chants the "Magnet Song" in a slow, steady voice.

Mag-net, mag-net — push, push, push.
Mag-net, mag-net — pull, pull, pull.

The moment is ripe for a rhythmic activity session to begin. The children are helped to complete their separate activities while the teacher moves some chairs out of the way, gets her tambourine out of the cupboard, and says, "Remember how we took the little magnets outdoors last week and rubbed them in the ground to pick up bits of iron from the dirt?" They remember, and then the teacher says, "I wonder what the earthworms thought when we were rubbing the magnets on top of their homes. Let's pretend we're all little worms trying to get away from the magnets." And she sings, keeping time with her tambourine:

Worms are crawl-ing, crawl-ing, crawl-ing,
Worms are crawl-ing under-neath the ground.
Crawl a-way from the mag-nets, mag-nets, mag-nets,
Crawl a-way from the mag-nets, mag-nets all a-round.

One by one, each child lies down on the floor and starts squirming around. A rhythmic activity session has begun.

Not all sessions fall into place so easily or unexpectedly; but each day, at one time or another, the teacher plays some rhythmic movement games with the group.

3 The Common Denominator Is Movement

The common denominator in each of the age groups is movement. The child moves; the group moves. The experienced teacher is alert to the changing moods and needs of each child as is evidenced by his movements and behavior. Taking her cues from these responses, she rearranges play areas or changes activities to harmonize with the varying needs as they arise. There is an easy rhythmic flow as the children move from one area to another. Furnishings have been so arranged as to create a pattern of movement from shelves to table, from storage to play areas, from front to back, and from side to side. The plan is for carrying and hauling—because that is the business of childhood.

Teachers are trained in the business of setting limits; but within these limits, the child is given freedom of activity according to his individual needs, abilities, and interests. Opportunities are given for alternating active and quiet periods, for individual play, and for group activities. Within this framework, the movement is rhythmic, the atmosphere is relaxed, and the activities are casual.

Although there is an underlying current of self-direction on the part of the child, this does not imply no teacher direction. It means the utilization of guidelines to point the way for the child, but not the pattern. These guidelines are important. They keep a child from exploding beyond set limits, and they keep group activities from disintegrating. Guidelines offer comfort and build confidence because they give the inexperienced child a starting point, and help him in learning to discriminate between random and meaningful experiences.

A child does not want to be told to "Do whatever you want to do." This only leads to confusion and frustration. He responds best to gentle guidance in which he is encouraged to interpret his ideas and actions in his own way. Creativity is nurtured; originality is applauded.

"But you said to do anything I wanted to."

4 The Rhythmic Activity Program

A goal-directed, child-oriented program of games and activities can range all the way from sitting quietly while swaying gently to an appropriate rhythm to a running-jumping activity involving use of the whole body. Through the stimulus of a steady rhythmic beat or simple rhymes and tunes, the child is led into a wide variety of creative activities based on natural developmental movements and growth patterns.

It is not anticipated that all the activities suggested in this program can be accomplished in any one year. The teacher should develop her own repertoire as the year progresses. A flexible attitude will permit her own creative forces, perhaps buried through long years of traditional conformity, to burst upon the horizon awaiting discovery through the eyes, thoughts, and actions of the young child.

In most of the activities, the child is free to explore and originate his own way of moving to the suggestions being offered. In some, however, direct imitation is called for to offer a different type of experience. Opportunities are also provided for pantomime and dramatization. After several months of a wide diversity of rhythmic movements, the child will respond well in "free dancing" to instrumental music, displaying grace and beauty.

Always choose a time when the children are well-rested and not overstimulated from a preceding activity. It might be immediately following a resting or story period; it might be shortly after arrival in the morning, following a period of quiet conversation, gradually leading up to the activity.

Always stop before fatigue develops. This might be in ten minutes or it could be half-an-hour or more. If the group is restless, channel the energy of the class into some of the gross motor activities such as running, galloping, and leaping. It might be well to move the entire activity to an outdoor area where there is ample freedom for rhythmic expression.

As the child experiences more and more rhythmic activities, he begins to want to express himself

TWO WAYS
APPROACHES TO TEACHING

ADULT-ORIENTED DIRECTIVES
(STEREOTYPED)

CHILD-ORIENTED GUIDES
(CREATIVE)

LEAD TO MOVEMENTS
WHICH ARE

Restricted		Flexible
Conforming		Originative
Stifled	VS.	Imaginative
Automatic		Improvised
Unvaried		Varied
Dependent		Interesting
Monotonous		Independent

WHICH IN TURN LEAD TO

Automatic experiences brought about
through learning by rote;
stifling of creative energy;
consumers and followers.

Flexible human beings who
will grow into sensitive and
mature adults so that they
become thinkers and leaders.

WHILE LEARNING ABOUT SELF AND SPACE
SPACE IN RELATION TO SELF
AND
SELF IN RELATION TO THE WORLD

DIRECTIONS

Room environment

TEACHER'S EDUCATIONAL BACKGROUND

TEACHER'S PREVIOUS EXPERIENCE

Child's previous experience

MECHANICAL DEVICES

Child's mood

TEACHER'S RIGIDITY

Child's home environment

TEACHER'S VOICE
authoritative—sharp

Child's voice

STANDARDIZED METHODS
always the same

Child's imagination

TEACHER'S EXPECTATIONS
chorus-line precision

TEACHER'S AMBITIONS
to impress parents

Note: One child managed to rebel—is it a wonder? But he'll be termed a "Behavior problem."

Rigid—Unimaginative—Mechanical—Standardized—Boring
The teacher's needs are so overwheming that her directions overwhelm the child.

SUGGESTIONS and GENTLE GUIDES

Child's Home Environment
and Cultural Heritage

Teacher

Child's previous
experience

Teacher

Interests of child

Teacher

Child's originality
and creativity

Child's own mood

Teacher

Child-oriented
room environment

Teacher

Mood of others
in the group

Teacher

Response of
each individual

Note protective presence
and personal involvement
of teacher.

Creative—Colorful—Original—Stimulating—Responsive

11

in song. Singing comes naturally for children and it is not taught formally in the nursery school. At first, short songs utilizing only two, three, or four tones may be improvised. Answering roll calls, imitating bird songs, or sighing like the wind will help the child "find his singing voice." These songs should be pitched high enough so that the child does not substitute the speaking voice for the singing voice. No accompaniment is needed for these short improvisations. The absence of accompaniment helps not only in developing "in-tuneness" and independence in singing, but it also allows for extemporaneous responses on the part of the child.

Later, nursery songs that have a steady beat can be introduced. These are excellent for developing auditory perception and aid in the improvement of motor coordination. Folk songs are also especially good, because of their catchy rhythms and repeated phrases. They do not need to be slowed down or simplified in deference to the child, since he can usually learn complicated songs easier than the average adult.

The text of most songs used in this book is generally sufficient to establish an appropriate tempo. In a few instances, however, suggestions for performance have been given. Nevertheless, the teacher should feel free to alter them in order to accommodate to the needs of a particular class or situation.

The tambourine is a most useful instrument to mark the beat as well as to set the tempo for the activities in *Creative Movement for the Developing Child*. It can produce a variety of sounds and requires little technique to play. The tambourine can be played slow or fast, and soft or loud; it can be an "elephant" or a "kitten." It can help a child to imagine a rainy day, falling leaves, or a circus parade. It can be "sleepy-time," too. Because of its versatility, many teachers call it the "Magic Tambourine." Since the tambourine can serve so many purposes, it is false economy to buy several toy ones instead of one really good instrument.

Using the tambourine does not preclude the use of other percussion instruments. Some teachers recommend a drum; but the advantage of the tambourine is that its ease of manipulation frees the teacher for a more complete involvement with the child during rhythmic activities.

Records should be considered as part of an enrichment program. They should definitely be used as an "added to" rather than an "in place of" part of the program. Records can be used for "active" listening as children perform well-defined rhythmic movements such as walking, running or skipping. They can also be used for "passive" listening in which the child listens to the music for pure enjoyment. This may take place during a resting period or as a preliminary to or follow-up of a rhythmic activity.

Great care must be taken not to become so dependent on records that the value of personal relationships is endangered. The young child needs much love; this means giving of one's self. Machines cannot give love — yet.

MOVEMENTS SEEN IN CHILDREN AT PLAY

Body Movements	Types of Games and Activities for Movement
Wriggling, squirming	No hands, standing, sitting, lying down.
Crawling	Abdomen touching floor: worms, caterpillars, snakes.
Creeping	Cat, dog, mouse, turtle, baby, tugboat, bugs.
Creeping (knees straight)	Spiders, lobsters, crabs.
Walking	Loud, soft, slow, fast, little, big, dolls, people.
Walking on tip-toes	Indian, baby is asleep, hiding.
Running, trotting	Big steps, little, wind, balloons, leaves.
Bouncing	Ball, jumping beans, Ten Little Indians.
Hopping	Alternate feet, Ten Little Indians.
Galloping	Horses, ponies.
Twirling	Dancer.
Spinning	Top — standing, sitting, lying down.
Scooting	On seat, abdomen, tugboat.
Jumping	Off of, over, onto; frog, kangaroo, grasshopper.
Bending, stooping	Bent-over man; touching toes.
Skating	Leaning forward; ice or roller.
Sliding	Sideways, back and forth.

Body Movements
(continued)

Shuffling	Shuffling man, old man.
Rocking	Sitting, lying down—abdomen or back.
Shaking	Standing, sitting; hula.
Turning	In one place, small circle, large circle, around.
Swaying	Alone, holding someone else's hands.
Dancing	Polka, hula, waltz, "free."
Balancing	Board, sideways, backwards, tight rope.
Climbing	Ladders, boxes, steps, hills, over.
Hiking	Up and down hills.
Playing ball	Throwing, catching, rolling.
Rolling over	Sideways, somersault.
Skipping	Ten Little Indians.

Types of Games and Activities for Movement
(continued)

Hand and Arm Movements

Swinging
Touching all parts of the body
Clapping
Slapping knees
Reaching
Stretching
Drooping
Swimming

Punching, boxing
Jumping rope
Pulling
Tugging
Lifting
Carrying
Waving
Sweeping, brushing

Picking up
Scrubbing
Shaking
Grasping, grabbing
Throwing, catching
Windmill
Patting
Pounding

Finger Movements

Pinching
Tickling
Touching
Rolling
Holding

Pointing
Tracing
Lacing
Winding
Snapping

Squeezing
Scratching
Pulling
Rubbing
Patting

Tapping
Folding
Tying
Cutting
Intertwining

Leg and Foot Movements

Kicking
Tapping toes
Tapping heels

Stamping
Wriggling toes
Standing on one foot

Bending knees only
Clicking heels together
Standing on tiptoes

Ways in Which To Move

Slowly
Quietly
Quickly

Loudly
Heavily
Silently

Hurriedly
Noisily
Sadly

Happily
Softly
Joyfully

Directions in Which To Move

Up
Down
Back
Forth
Backward
Forward
Across

Sideways
The other way
Over
Under
Above
Below
In a circle

Underneath
Beneath
Between
To the side of
To the other side of
To the back of
In front of

15

5 The Non-participant

What about the child who does not readily participate in the activities as described in *Creative Movement for the Developing Child*? He may need time to identify with the program, or he may just prefer the role of an observer. If he enjoys watching and listening, then he may be participating in the way which best meets his needs.

Give the child plenty of time, and handle each individual with patience and gentleness. Above all, never force or coerce him to participate in an activity as this would probably have a detrimental psychological effect.

Stand next to the child and, as the others respond to the rhythm, swing his hand with yours in a relaxed and unobtrusive manner.

Sit next to him. Hold his hand or put your arm around his shoulder, and sway gently from side to side in response to the rhythm. Your protective arm may provide him with the security he needs to encourage active participation.

Suggest that he clap his hands while the others are moving about:

Sing "Rock-a-bye Baby" while everyone holds and rocks an imaginary baby. The children do not sense themselves as moving, but rather the baby. The non-participant may automatically start moving with the group in this way. This activity lends itself very well to pantomiming when the cradle falls and everyone looks so sad.

Since resting is a daily routine in which everyone participates, a non-participant may join in resting games because he is used to responding during rest periods.

The use of songs in moving from one area to another may encourage the non-participant to join the next activity.

If a child continues as a non-participant, but is in need of perceptual-motor activities, the really creative teacher uses all her ingenuity in improvising special projects to provide the needed training.

6   Crawling (Part I)

A six-month-old child who is developing normally has usually achieved a certain amount of trunk control, having learned to turn his body from side to side and to turn himself over from either his abdomen or his back. He has also learned by now to propel himself by crawling to get from one place to another. As the infant moves himself forward on the floor or the bed, the resultant sensation of his body against the surface on which he is moving is registered on his brain. This sensation of whole body movement on a flat surface may be reflected later in his ability to write on a flat surface with fluidity of movement.

Most children in nursery school respond to activities which take place on the floor. It seems to impart a sense of security, taking the child back to the warmth and comfort of his infancy and renewing early tactile and kinesthetic memories.

Since crawling is so basic to the natural development of a child's movements, it is used as a point of departure for this entire rhythmic movement program. Introductory activities which lead to crawling depend on wiggling, squirming movements that employ whole body movements.

Discuss earthworms. If possible, bring some live earthworms into the classroom. Talk about how they live and how they dig tunnels in the ground by eating the dirt. Is it warm or cold under the ground? Is it light or dark? Why does the worm come out when it rains? Let the children discover how earthworms move. Let them discover that they have to wiggle because they have no arms or legs.

Suggest that everyone get down on the floor and see how it feels to be a worm. Improvise a chant to "Worms Are Crawling" and, to the beat of your tambourine, sing it as the "worms" crawl at random around the room. Adjust the rhythm and tempo according to the children's natural movements.

WORMS ARE CRAWLING

Chant
Tambourine

Worms are crawl-ing, crawl-ing, crawl-ing,
Worms are crawl-ing, crawl-ing all a-round.

Mak-ing lit-tle tun-nels, tun-nels, tun-nels,
Mak-ing lit-tle tun-nels under-neath the ground.

Spoken (through a rolled-up magazine to give a muffled sound)

Lit-tle worms, can you hear me under there?
Is it hot or cold under the ground?
Is it light or dark?
I think it is go-ing to rain.

Chant

Rain, rain, rain-ing, and the worms are crawl-ing,
out of the tun-nels, up a-bove the ground.

WIGGLY WORMS

Tune: *The Farmer in the Dell*
Tambourine

Oh, wig-gly, wig-gly worms
Are squirm-ing all a-round,
Squig-gle, squig-gle, wig-gle worms,
Crawl in and out the ground.

Substitute "snakes" for "worms" as a variant to this activity. Remind the children that snakes usu-ally move much faster than worms.

18

MR. SNAKE

Tune: *Oats, Peas, Beans*
Lively

Wig-gly, wig-gly, wig-gly snake,
Crawl-ing, crawl-ing all a-round,
Oh, he's a slip-per-y, slip-per-y snake,
Crawl-ing, crawl-ing on the ground.

BOBBY SNAKE

(Substitute each child's name.)
Chant
Adjust tempo to movement of each child.

Oh, Bob-by snake is crawl-ing, crawl-ing,
Crawl-ing right up to me.

SNAKE GAME

The teacher says, "Help! Help! Look at all the snakes crawling around my feet. Go away, snakes. Go away!" (Sometimes they do and sometimes they don't. But it's always fun to play make-believe with the teacher.)

7 Crawling (Part II)

Worms and snakes crawl with a wiggling movement. Introduce other creatures that use their "arms" to pull the body forward and the "feet" to push with.

The salamander is a little-known amphibian that makes a wonderful pet. It is easy to take care of and fun to observe. Put it in an aquarium with a rock to climb on. Help the children to see how it crawls in two different rhythmic patterns. In the water, the salamander moves in a homolateral pattern. That is, the right "arm and leg" move forward while the left "arm and leg" are stretched to the rear and vice versa. On land, however, the little salamander changes its movement to a true cross-pattern, in which the opposite "arm and leg" move at the same time. Since the child should develop a good cross-pattern movement, the "Salamander" may be used very effectively to teach this movement. As the teacher performs the chant, she should mark a steady beat, not the rhythmic pattern, on the tambourine. No explanation need be made to the child; his natural instinct will soon be activated and his movement will automatically coordinate with the steady beat.

SALAMANDER
Tambourine

Funny sal-a-man-der,
I see you.
Crawl-ing on your tum-my,
A-one and a-two.
First you reach with one hand,
Then with the oth-er,
Each time a hand goes out,
You push a lit-tle fur-ther.

The "Alligator Game," like many others in *Creative Movement for the Developing Child*, is planned as an ego-building activity. The child feels very powerful when he is scaring the teacher.

ALLIGATOR GAME

I was walking in the jungle far, far away. I didn't know where I was going, so I became lost. But I knew if I crossed the river, I would get home. As I started across the river, I saw an alligator. Then I saw another . . . and another . . . and another. How will I ever get across the river? Help! Help! Help! (*At this point, you may start dodging the swarming "alligators" which will be trying to get you. You may have to climb up on a chair.*)

CROCODILES
Chant
Lively

Hey, hey, hey there, croc-o-dile,
Stay a-way from me.
Hey, hey, hey there, croc-o-dile,
Swim out to the sea.

Hey, hey, hey there, croc-o-dile,
Please go the oth-er way,
Hey, hey, hey there, croc-o-dile,
You're chas-ing me a-way.

8 Creeping

When the child is about six to eight months of age, he learns to raise his abdomen from the floor and to support himself with his hands and knees. Then he begins to propel himself forward in that position, that is, to creep. If he has had many opportunities to move about freely on his stomach in the crawling movement, he will now be able to develop a good cross-pattern creep quickly. Many nursery school children cannot cross-pattern creep. In discussing this with their parents, it was found that some of these children did very little crawling or creeping before ten or eleven months of age. By that time, they were usually walking. Some walked as early as seven or eight months, thus skipping lightly over intermediate stages of motor development. While the child is learning to function in a bilateral or two-sided movement, he is also learning to use both eyes "in concert." As his hands move rhythmically, his eyes pick up that movement and visual-motor perceptual growth results.

In addition to the creeping activities given below, the child may be given many opportunities to creep in his play at school. Tunnels may be formed by tipping over chairs in a row. Cover the chairs with a blanket for additional motivation.

Cats are familiar animals to the child, and "creeping like a cat" comes very easy. Discussions about cats make good introductions to chants, songs, and games. This cat is looking for a mouse. How will she creep? Slow or fast. Cats are very quiet when they creep; but when they "talk," everyone can hear them.

Let some in the group be "cats." Others may be "mice." The "cats" can hide from each other, chase each other, or the "cats" can catch the "mice." Sometimes a third group, pretending to be "dogs," may chase the "cats" to save the "mice."

THE BIG GRAY CAT
Tambourine

The big gray cat goes
MEEEEEE-OWWWWW, MEEEEEE-OWWWW,
The big gray cat goes
MEEEEEE-OWWWWW, MEEEEEE-OWWWW,

MAMA CAT
Tune: *Oats, Peas, Beans*

See the big fat ma-ma cat,
See the big fat ma-ma cat,
She creeps a-long all through the house,
Look-ing for a lit-tle mouse.

THREE BLIND MICE
Lively

Three blind mice, three blind mice,
See how they run, see how they run.
They all ran af-ter the farm-er's wife,
She cut off their tails with a carv-ing knife,
Did ev-er you see such a sight in your life,
As three blind mice.

A small turtle was brought to school, and it was allowed to walk around the room. The class discussed the turtle's movements and decided to make up a turtle dance. It had to be very slow, because that is the way a turtle moves. This is an excellent activity for the development of cross-pattern creeping. Slow movements are much more difficult to do than fast ones; thus, "Turtle" provides an opportunity for practice which will lead to improvement in the ability to perform this activity.

TURTLE
Tune: *Twinkle, Twinkle, Little Star*
Very slow

Tur-tle, tur-tle, where are you?
Oh, you are so slow, slow, slow.
First, one hand and then the oth-er,
That's what makes you go, go, go.

Hide your wink-y, wink-y head,
Then you can-not see, see, see.
Tur-tle, tur-tle, peek-a-boo,
Peek-a-boo at me, me, me.

Turtle activities can later be expanded to include discussions of snails and a comparison of their "houses" and movements. Which moves slower? Does the snail crawl or creep? What makes him move?

SNAIL

Tune: *Same as "Turtle" song.*

Lit-tle snail, Oh, where are you?
In your shell, you go so slow.
You've no hands; you have no feet,
What can ev-er make you go?

Hide your wink-y lit-tle head,
And you can-not see, see, see.
Lit-tle snail, you go so slow,
But you are such fun to show.

Another favorite creeping activity of children is pretending they are "tug boats." This game can be varied in many ways. Some children may be tug boats; others may be the big ships. Maybe some "tug boats" can blow their "whistles" to warn other ships to keep out of the way.

TUG BOAT

Tune: *Twinkle, Twinkle, Little Star*

Lit-tle boat, come out to sea.
Chug-chug, chug-chug, fol-low me.
Pull big boats out in the bay,
Oth-er boats must pull away.
Tug-tug, tug-tug, tug-tug-tug,
Oth-er boats will pull a-way.
Lit-tle boat, come out to sea.
Chug-chug, chug-chug, fol-low me.

THE DIGGING MOLE STORY

Do you remember when we talked about earthworms? We found that they live in the ground. They make their tunnels by eating the dirt as they crawl along. Do you know what a mole is? It looks something like a big rat. It lives in the ground, but it doesn't eat the dirt to dig its tunnel. It digs its tunnel with its two hands. It digs the dirt loose with its paws and pushes itself forward with its back feet. I wonder what it would be like to live in a mole tunnel. I'll sing a song about the mole and you can did a tunnel while I sing. (Sing through a paper rolled up to form a megaphone. This will give a sound as if you were underground.)

THE DIGGING MOLE

Tune: *My Darling Clementine*

Mis-ter mole, mis-ter mole,
Mis-ter mole, oh how you dig,
Dig a tun-nel, dig a tun-nel,
Dig a tun-nel through the ground.

Dig a tun-nel, dig a tun-nel,
With your hands, and with your feet,
Dig a tun-nel, dig a tun-nel,
Through the dirt in-to the ground.

9 Creeping on All Fours

The next stage in normal development of locomotion is creeping on "all fours," that is, on the hands and feet, rather than on the hands and knees. Frequently this step is omitted completely, because the child has learned to stand alone by this time and is encouraged to walk upright. Nevertheless, sometimes a child of about one year of age will be observed running rapidly across the floor on his hands and feet. This movement is excellent for general muscular development of the legs and back, and it is a healthy preliminary to walking in an erect manner.

Discuss the long legs of spiders. How many legs do they have? Do they have knees? Have you ever seen a crab walk? Do crabs have long legs like spiders? How do they walk differently from spiders? Let's see if we can be spiders and crabs when we walk.

SPIDERS
Chant
Slow, deliberate

The great big spi-der's walk-ing on the ground.
The great big spi-der's walk-ing all a-round
Walk-ing, walk-ing, walk-ing all a-round.

CRABS
Chant

Oh, when I go down to the beach,
What do you think I see?
Crabs a-walking, crabs a-walking,
Walk-ing af-ter me.

Although most children will imitate a bear by walking upright, it can be explained that they can stand upright although they usually run on all fours.

THE BEAR
Tune: *Farmer in the Dell*

Oh, here comes the bear,
Oh, here comes the bear,
Bend-ing o-ver in the mid-dle,
Here comes the bear.

Oh, see how he walks,
Oh, see how he walks,
Like a bro-ken ted-dy bear,
Oh, see how he walks.

Since this is such an excellent physical exercise for the young child, he should be encouraged to prolong the activity. In this, and other games, you can motivate variations by making obstacle courses —tables to go under and blocks or other objects to crawl over. Another variation is to have the bear (or other animal) walk along a 1' x 12' board placed on the floor.

10 Walking

As the child's strength and skills develop, he learns to walk in an upright position. At first, the walking movement is a combination of body movements which are not yet synchronized. With repeated practice, however, he gradually achieves greater balance and is able to walk with rhythmic coordination. By the time the child has entered nursery school, walking has become so generalized a motor activity that it does not require conscious thought for its performance.

The child now expands freely on his original movements, enlarging the number of activities in which he can participate. This tends to further his understanding of his relationship to space.

Children like to talk about babies. Have a child demonstrate how his little baby brother or sister is learning to walk. Talk about how the little baby holds his hands outward and up to control his balance and how he walks with his feet wide apart. Can your baby brother or sister run?

BABY

Tune: *Mary Had a Little Lamb*

Lit-tle ba-by walk-ing now, walk-ing now,
    walk-ing now,
Lit-tle ba-by walk-ing now, walk-ing now so slow.

Lit-tle ba-by talk-ing now, talk-ing now,
    talk-ing now,
Lit-tle ba-by talk-ing now, talk-ing now so slow.

Spoken

"Ma-ma! Ma-ma!"

LITTLE MAN, BIG MAN GAME

Spoken

Do you know what a little baby did when he was learning to walk? He ate his breakfast every day. He ate his lunch every day. And he ate his dinner every day, too. He started growing and growing and growing. Soon, he was a man. But he wasn't a big man. At first, he was just a little man.

Chant

The lit-tle ti-ny man takes lit-tle ti-ny steps.

Tambourine

Lit-tle ti-ny steps, lit-tle ti-ny steps.
The lit-tle ti-ny man takes lit-tle ti-ny steps.
The lit-tle ti-ny man takes lit-tle ti-ny steps.

Spoken

He kept on eating and drinking all his milk. He went to school, and he learned many things. He grew bigger and bigger. All of a sudden, he was a great big man. He was so big that when he walked, he took big, giant steps.

Chant

The great big man takes great big steps.

Tambourine

The great big man takes big, gi-ant steps.
(Repeat)

This game can be varied in many ways. Alternate the lines of "little tiny man" and "great big man" without missing a beat. Divide the children into groups, some playing the part of "tiny men" and others playing "big men." Alternate the two songs and have the children listen for the appropriate time for them to move.

Make up new verses, such as "The fun-ny crook-ed man takes fun-ny crook-ed steps," or "The big fat man takes big fat steps." The children should be encouraged to make up verses, too.

THE GENTLE GIANT
Chant
Slow, deliberate

What animals take big steps? Do some animals take very big, giant steps? Do they walk fast or slow?

A-one and a-two, and a-one and a-two,
I'm a gen-tle gi-ant and I won't hurt you.

DINOSAUR
Chant
Slow, deliberate

Here comes a di-no-saur walk-ing down the street,
I think he is some-one I do not want to meet.

ELEPHANT GAME
Improvise tune
Tambourine, slow

If I were an e-le-phant,
I would so hap-py be,
I would swing my trunk and say,
"Come a-long with me."

11 Running

As the muscular strength of the child increases, he gradually learns to run. At first he runs stiffly, but with great pleasure and enthusiasm. He should be given many opportunities to practice running activities in order to increase the ease with which he is able to move through space. Activities such as floating or flying can be utilized to provide interesting games for children to develop facility in running.

The wind is rhythmic. It is always moving. The wind blows through trees and makes the leaves shake. Strong winds can blow paper, weeds, and sand. Have the children be a "big wind" and blow everything out of their way.

FLYING THROUGH THE AIR
Tune: *Mary Had a Little Lamb*

The wind is blow-ing all a-round,
All a-round, all a-round.
The wind is blow-ing all a-round,
All a-round the air.

CLOUDS ARE FLOATING
Tune: *Frère Jacques*

Clouds are float-ing, clouds are float-ing,
Up so high, up so high,
Float-ing up a-bove us, float-ing up a-bove us,
In the sky, in the sky.

THE WINDS AND THE CLOUDS

Low, stormy tone

A storm was com-ing. The wind was blow-ing hard.
It was "swoosh-ing" through the trees.
The clouds were get-ting dark and heav-y.
Wind was blow-ing the clouds all a-round.
It was blow-ing and dark and storm-y.
Wooooo . . . wooooo . . . woooo.

Children like to talk about birds. Since birds are a part of our everyday environment, children can observe many thing about them. Some birds sing beautiful songs; but they do not sing like we do. Other birds just make noises. The crow only says "Caw-caw-caw." Baby birds say "Peep-peep-peep." Flying like a bird helps develop muscular coordination for running.

FLY AWAY

Tune: *Row, Row, Row*

Fly, fly, fly a-way,
Hap-py as can be.
Oh, fly, fly, fly a-way,
Then fly back to me.

SEA GULLS ARE FLYING

Improvise tune
Tambourine

When the sea gulls are fly-ing,
They wave their arms at me.
They fly so high, up in the sky
And way on out to sea.
Fly, fly, fly a-way
Way on out to sea.
Fly, fly, fly a-way
Wave your wings at me.

When children are flying, they usually want to continue this activity. This movement gives children an overall feeling of exhilaration. What other things fly? There are butterflies, bees, and many other insects; there are also mechanical things that fly such as airplanes and helicopters.

BUTTERFLYING

Improvise tune
Tambourine

Flying, flying, but-ter-flying,
All a-cross the sky.
Flying, flying, but-ter-flying,
Up so ver-y high!

34

AIRPLANES

Tune: *Frère Jacques*

Air-planes run-ning, air-planes hum-ming,
ZZZZZ ZZZZZZZZZZZ ZZZZZ, ZZZZZZZZZ ZZZZ.
See them fly-ing high-er,
Watch them fly-ing low-er,
ZZZZZZZZZZZZZZZZ, ZZZZZZZZZZZZZZZZ.

HELICOPTERS

Tune: *Frère Jacques*

He-li-cop-ters, he-li-cop-ters,
ZZZZZZZZZZZZZZZZZZZ, ZZZZZZZZZZ ZZZZZ.
See them fly-ing high-er,
Watch them fly-ing low-er,
ZZZZZ ZZZZZZZZZ, ZZZZZZZZZZZZZZZZZZZZZ.

TRANSPORTATION GAME

One adult stands with the children at one end of a large running area, such as a parking lot or a playground. Another adult stands at the other end of the area and shouts, "Airplanes fly-ing! Airplanes flying!" The children "fly" to her like airplanes. Then they are called back by the other adult with, "Horses running! Horses running!" And they run to her imitating horses. Continue the game with helicopters flying, automobiles rac-ing, boats sailing, trains chugging, and so on.

12 Jumping and Leaping

Children depend very much on jumping and leaping as a means of emotional expression. A child jumps for joy! He jumps when he is impatient, curious or excited. He jumps up and down when he doesn't get his own way. Jumping is one of the most natural movements for children.

The movements required for leaping are similar to those needed for jumping. A child who learns to jump with dexterity will probaby have little difficulty in learning to leap.

In planning activities for jumping, include those which encourage the child to jump from one place to another, to jump over some object, to jump up onto something, and to jump down from something. He can be given cardboard boxes or boards to jump over. There can be an imaginary river, a pattern in the tile, or a crack in the sidewalk. Give him opportunities to jump from a standing position or to run and jump.

As the child increases his skill in jumping, he will be developing his whole body balance and overall physical coordination, along with the development of visual-motor perception which accompanies such activities.

LITTLE GRASSHOPPER
Tune: Chant or adapt to *La Cucaracha*

Lit-tle grass-hop-per, lit-tle grass-hop-per,
Jump-ing all o-ver the land,
Lit-tle grass-hop-per, lit-tle grass-hop-per,
Jump-ing right in-to my hand.
Lit-tle grass-hop-per, lit-tle grass-hop-per,
Jump-ing, jump-ing far a-way,
Lit-tle grass-hop-per, lit-tle grass-hop-per,
Come a-gain an-oth-er day.

KALAMAZOO, THE KANGAROO

Tune: *Old MacDonald Had a Farm*

Kal-a-ma-zoo, the kan-ga-roo,
See what I can do.
I jump as far as a mo-tor car.
You can do it, too.
Oh, sing a jump-jump,
Oh, sing a bump-bump,
Here a jump, there a bump,
Ev'ry-where a jump-bump,
Kal-a-ma-zoo, the kan-ga-roo,
Go-ing to Kal-ka-roo.

Kal-a-ma-zoo, the kan-ga-roo,
See what I can do.
In one short week, I jump a creek,
You can do it, too.
Oh, sing a jump-jump,
Oh, sing a bump-bump,
Here a jump, there a bump,
Ev'ry-where a jump-bump,
Kal-a-ma-zoo, the kan-ga-roo,
Go-ing to Kal-ka-roo.

"Grasshopper Song" is a good activity to use outdoors. Do not try to teach each child to play leapfrog. Usually, children prefer to jump alone.

GRASSHOPPER SONG

Tune: *Battle Hymn of the Republic*

One grass-hop-per jumped right o-ver
The oth-er grass-hop-per's back,
The oth-er grass-hop-per jumped right o-ver
An-oth-er grass-hop-per's back.
And the oth-er grass-hop-per jumped right over
The oth-er grass-hop-per's back.
Jumped right over his back!

Sway to and fro on these lines

Oh, they were on-ly play-ing leap-frog,
Oh, they were on-ly play-ing leap-frog,
Oh, they were on-ly play-ing leap-frog,
Jump-ing right o-ver the oth-er grass-hop-per's back.

JACK BE NIMBLE GAME

Improvise props. Make up additional verses.

Jack be nim-ble, Jack be quick,
Jack jump o-ver the can-dle-stick.

Jack be nim-ble, quick as a fox,
Jack jump o-ver this lit-tle box.

Jack be nim-ble, Jack cut a ca-per,
Jack jump over this piece of pa-per.

Jack be nim-ble, Jack be fair,
Jack jump o-ver this lit-tle chair.

Jack be nim-ble, and bright as a star,
Stand up and jump ver-y wide and far.

Part of the fun in doing a wide variety of creative movement activities is in the reinforcement of concepts resulting from them. With some practice, the observant teacher will soon find herself continuously interweaving the rhythmic activities with some learning experience which had taken place previously. The "Popcorn Game" is an example.

The teacher brought a glass-topped popper to school, and she allowed the children to use it in class. The children discovered that the size of the popcorn grew from little to big; the color changed from yellow to white; the texture changed from hard and shiny to soft and dull; and heat made the corn pop.

Several days later, the teacher suggested that the children make up a popcorn dance. They were enthusiastic, and had so many ideas and so much fun that before they were finished they had improvised four songs to which they hopped, jumped, and slid all around.

POPCORN GAME
First tune: *I'm a Little Teapot*

I'm a lit-tle pop-corn in a pot,
Heat me up and watch me pop,
When I get all fat and white then I'm done,
Pop-ping corn is lots of fun.

Since some of the kernels didn't pop, the teacher suggested that she would make the fire a little hotter and see if the unpopped kernels would pop.

No tune

Lit-tle ker-nels so still and qui-et,
Lit-tle ker-nels that did-n't get white,
Lit-tle ker-nels that just did-n't pop,
Lit-tle ker-nels ly-ing in the pot.

Tune: *Row, Row, Row*

Pop, pop, pop my corn,
Pop it big and white,
Pop-ping, pop-ping, pop-ping, pop-ping,
'Til it is just right.

Tune: *Jim Crack Corn*

Jim crack corn and I don't care,
I'm pop-ping right up in the air,
I'm pop-ping up and I'm pop-ping down,
And I'm pop-ping right all o-ver the town.

13   Teacher-child Involvement

Close involvement between the teacher and the children leads to more effective teaching that results in more meaningful learning experiences. It is hoped that the teacher will really be having as much fun as the children, and that she will not hesitate to involve herself directly in each activity with no in-between barriers.

An inexperienced teacher may be reluctant to be put in such a position. In actual fact, however, direct participation in such a situation results in stronger teacher-child bonds. By being so closely involved with the teacher on his own level, the child learns more easily to respond to the teacher on her level.

Occasionally, the teacher can be a full participant in a game. Games such as "The Walk in the Jungle" actually place the child in a more important role than the teacher, building his ego-strength and self-image. A teacher who can accept her role in such games, without constantly reminding the children that she is the teacher and therefore must "command respect," will immediately establish rapport with the class.

To prepare for "The Walk in the Jungle," small chairs or hollow blocks are placed in a semi-circle to represent trees. The teacher acts out her part as she relates the story. The children, on cues from the teacher, join in the dramatization. Each child chooses to be a lion, a leopard, or a tiger and "hides" up in a tree. This game can be varied by having the teacher reverse the roles of walker and animals with the children.

THE WALK IN THE JUNGLE

One day, I was walking in a jungle in a faraway land. It was very still and quiet. I couldn't hear any one. I couldn't see anyone. I wondered where all the animals were that lived in the jungle. I walked very slowly and I looked all around. I looked behind the bushes. (*Look behind the chairs at one end of the semi-circle.*) I looked behind the trees. (*Look at the other end of the circle.*) I looked behind me. (*Look slowly in a complete circle.*) I still couldn't see any animals. But then I felt that someone was watching me. (*Get very dramatic.*) Who was it? What was it? I still couldn't see anyone. (*Get more and more dramatic.*) Then I looked up into the trees. And I saw who was watching me. There were lions and tigers and leopards there. They looked as if they were ready to leap at me. (*Get more excited.*) I looked around quickly for a place to hide. I found a place that was just right. (*Tip a small table on its side to make a cave.*) But before I could get to the cave, the animals began to growl. I was afraid to move. (*Remind the animals not to growl so loud that they won't be able to hear the story.*) They growled louder and LOUDER and L O U D E R. (*Run around the room toward the cave as soon as the children leap. They will "get you" anyway, but that is part of the fun.*)

14 Galloping and Skipping

Walking, running, jumping, and leaping are the basic natural movements which actually move the body through space. All other locomotor movements are either a combination or a variation of these. When a child has achieved a certain amount of skill in these basic movements, he is ready for more complicated experiences. The two which will be considered here are galloping and skipping.

Galloping is fairly easy for a young child to perform since it is a unilateral activity, using only one side of the body. It combines the movements of walking and leaping, and the child is quick to grasp its rhythmic possibilities.

A natural introduction to galloping movements is to talk about horses. The child or the teacher can bring pictures of horses from home. Many children will have toy horses which they can share. Discuss the colors and sizes of different horses. What is a colt? How can you tell the difference between a horse and a pony? Can you make a noise like a horse? A horse can walk, run, trot, prance, and gallop. Which way is the fastest?

In improvising galloping games, have the "horses" gallop slow, fast, loud, and soft. Let them start out by galloping loud and gradually getting softer to give the impression of being farther and farther away. Occasionally use sticks for make-believe "horses." Stop to drink water and eat some hay. Suggest that the child try galloping with the other "hoof" in the lead.

GALLOP AND GALLOP MY PONY
Tune: *Pawpaw Patch*

Gal-lop and gal-lop and gal-lop my po-ny,
Gal-lop and gal-lop and gal-lop my po-ny,
Gal-lop and gal-lop and gal-lop my po-ny,
Gal-lop and gal-lop and gal-lop a-way.

GALLOPING HORSES
Tune: *Ten Little Indians*

Gal-lop-ing, gal-lop-ing, gal-lop-ing hors-es,
Gal-lop-ing, gal-lop-ing, gal-lop-ing hors-es,
Gal-lop-ing, gal-lop-ing, gal-lop-ing hors-es,
Gal-lop-ing all the way.

Skipping, although also based on a combination of two natural movements, walking and hopping, is a much more difficult achievement for the young child. Skipping is a bilateral movement, definitely requiring equal use of both sides of the body. Since the young child is still in the process of achieving laterality, an early approach to the activity must be as simple as possible.

It is suggested that the basic movements for skipping be presented separately and in sequence over a period of two or three years. Vary the process according to the needs of a partciular group or a particular child. Once learned, skipping is frequently used to express a feeling of happiness and well-being.

SKIPPING SONGS
Tune: *Ten Little Indians*

Two-three year olds

Lift one foot and then the oth-er,
Lift one foot and then the oth-er,
Lift one foot and then the oth-er,
Ten lit-tle In-di-an boys.

Three-four year olds

Hop on one foot, then on the oth-er,
Hop on one foot, then on the oth-er,
Hop on one foot, then on the oth-er,
Ten lit-tle In-di-an boys.

Four-five year olds

Walk and hop and walk and hop now,
Walk and hop and walk and hop now,
Walk and hop and walk and hop now,
Ten lit-tle In-di-an boys.

Use when ready at teacher's discretion

Skip and skip and skip, lit-le In-di-ans,
Skip and skip and skip, lit-le In-di-ans,
Skip and skip and skip, lit-le In-di-ans,
Skip lit-tle In-di-an boys.

SKIP TO MY LOU
Tune: *Skip to My Lou*
Tambourine

Skip, skip, skip to my Lou,
Skip, skip, skip to my Lou,
Skip, skip, skip to my Lou,
Skip to my Lou, my dar-ling.

15 Whole Body Movements

Whole body movements are those which do not transport the body through space, but which involve the use of the whole body. Included in this group are such movements as bending, bouncing, pulling, pushing, rocking, shaking, stretching, stooping and wiggling. They are basic to the development of flexible posture and fluidity of motor control, and they lead to the performance of higher skills. As dexterity in these movements is achieved, they are combined with locomotor movements to encompass an ever-increasing range of rhythmic activities.

The teacher must observe each child carefully, and learn to "feel" his need for either more simple or more complex games. The child is given constant encouragement to originate his own activities and express his own ideas. However, if the teacher observes he may be having difficulty in performing a certain type of movement, she should be ready to help him in whatever way he may need. Sometimes this may be direct physical assistance; however, techniques such as a slight change of wording in a song, a simplification of a certain rhythmic pattern, or a modification of the music will emphasize the type of response which is the goal of a particular activity.

The following songs make an excellent introduction to the development of whole body movements. They are easily combined with locomotor activities and should be interchanged one with another.

THE BENT OVER MAN

Chant
Lively

I'm a bent o-ver, bent o-ver, bent o-ver man,
I try to stand just as straight as I can.
But all I can do is bend and bend,
Be-cause I'm a bent o-ver, bent o-ver man.

I'm a sway-ing, sway-ing, sway-ing man,
I try to stand just as still as I can.
But all I can do is sway back and forth,
Be-cause I'm a sway-ing, sway-ing man.

I'm a side-ways, side-ways, side-ways man,
I try to stand just as still as I can,
But all I can do is slide side-ways,
Be-cause I'm a side-ways, side-ways man.

I'm a smil-ing, smil-ing, smil-ing man,
I try to look just as sad as I can.
But all I can do is smile and smile,
Be-cause I'm a smil-ing, smil-ing man.

I'm a head-shak-ing, head-shak-ing, head-shak-ing
    man,
I try to hold my head just as still as I can.
But all I can do is shake and shake,
Be-cause I'm a head-shak-ing, head-shak-ing man.

THIS OLD MAN

Tune: *This Old Man*

This old man, he can shake,
Shake, shake, shake while bak-ing a cake,
Nick nack pad-dy-wack, give your dog a bone,
Shak-ing, shak-ing all the way home.

This old man, he can kick,
Kick, kick, kick, kick just for a trick,
Nick nack pad-dy-wack, give your dog a bone,
Kick-ing, kick-ing all the way home.

This old man, he can twist,
Twist, twist, twist while shak-ing his fist,
Nick nack pad-dy-wack, give your dog a bone,
Twist-ing, twist-ing all the way home.

This old man, he can sway,
Sway, sway, sway while try-ing to play,
Nick nack pad-dy-wack, give your dog a bone,
Sway-ing, sway-ing all the way home.

This old man, he can point,
Point, point, point all o-ver the joint,
Nick nack pad-dy-wack, give your dog a bone,
Point-ing, point-ing all the way home.

Running in place

This old man, he can run,
Run, run, run, run just for fun,
Nick nack pad-dy-wack, give your dog a bone,
Run-ning, run-ning all the way home.

This old man, he can slide,
Slide, slide, slide from side to side,
Nick nack pad-dy-wack, give your dog a bone,
Slid-ing, slid-ing all the way home.

This old man, he can jump,
Jump, jump, jump, jump o-ver a bump,
Nick nack pad-dy-wack, give your dog a bone,
Jump-ing, jump-ing all the way home.

SPINNING, TWIRLING

Tune: *Row, Row, Row*
Children standing

Spin, spin, spin your top,
Twirl it all a-round,
Spin it, twirl it, spin it, twirl it,
Throw it on the ground.

Children seated

Spin, spin, spin your top,
Twirl it all a-round,
Spin it, twirl it, spin it, twirl it,
Throw it on the ground.

Children lying on the ground
(first on stomachs, then on backs)

Spin, spin, spin your top,
Twirl it all a-round,
Spin-ning, spin-ning, twirl-ing, twirl-ing,
Turn it 'round and 'round.

Spinning may also be done in a stooping position although it is a much more difficult activity. Vary this activity by playing "statues." The teacher twirls one child at a time and then lets go. The child "freezes" in whatever position he lands. Later, the children may take turns twirling each other around.

ROWING AND ROCKING
Tune: *Row, Row, Row*
(Have children sit on floor, facing a partner. They hold hands as they rock back and forth.)

Row, row, row, your boat,
Gent-ly down the stream,
Mer-ri-ly, mer-ri-ly, mer-ri-ly, mer-ri-ly,
Life is but a dream.

Rock, rock, rock your boat,
Gent-ly down the stream,
Mer-ri-ly, mer-ri-ly, mer-ri-ly, mer-ri-ly,
Life is but a dream.

16 Kinesthetic Awareness

Throughout the rhythmic movement activities, the child is also developing the sensory-motor process and an awareness of the capabilities of his body to perform deliberate movements at will. He develops a kinesthetic awareness which helps him to understand the uses of various parts of his body in movements. While he is learning what his body can do outwardly, he is also growing in the knowledge of how it can feel inwardly. This new concept leads to a greater awareness of balance, spatial relationships, and the child's own self.

Kinesthetic awareness may begin with such simple experiences as reaching and stretching, similar to those movements made by an infant during the earliest weeks of its life. For tactile experiences, the type of surface used in these activities should be as varied as possible. Sometimes they should be performed on a hard floor, sometimes on a rug, and sometimes out-of-doors on a grassy area. In fact, moving such an activity out-of-doors will increase space perception as well as sensitivity to living, growing surfaces.

In preparation for the following games, the area should be as clear of objects as possible, to allow sufficient room for each child to perform freely and unencumbered. The teacher should help each child find a space where he will be out of reach of any other child.

REACHING WITH MY ARMS
Chant
Soft and quiet

I reach with my one arm, then with the oth-er,
I reach for my sis-ter, I reach for my broth-er,
I reach for the ceil-ing, I reach for the wall,
I reach for so man-y things, I reach for them all.

REACHING, STRETCHING
Chant

Reach-ing, stretch-ing, reach-ing, stretch-ing,
Stretch my arms way out,
Reach-ing, stretch-ing, reach-ing, stretch-ing,
Reach-ing all a-bout.

Softer and quieter

Reach-ing, stretch-ing, reach-ing, stretch-ing,
Stretch my legs way out,
Reach-ing, stretch-ing, reach-ing, stretch-ing,
Reach-ing all a-bout.

The teacher can then say, "Now let's do that again. But this time, I'm not going to say the words. Just pretend that I'm saying them as you reach and stretch. If you listen very carefully, you will be able to hear your muscles inside of you stretching."

The next step is to repeat the process, but this time with the suggestion that the child keep his eyes closed. "Now, you'll be able really to hear yourself move."

Encourage the children to move sideways as you sing "Roll, Little Football." This movement should be similar to a baby's early movements. Suggest that the child listen to his body as he rolls. The rolling activity can be varied by having the children close their eyes while performing this movement or rolling like a wagon.

ROLL, LITTLE FOOTBALL
Tune: *Little Red Wagon*

Roll, lit-tle foot-ball, roll and roll,
Roll, lit-tle foot-ball, roll and roll,
First your head and then your legs,
Roll, lit-tle foot-ball, roll and roll.

ROLLING ALONG
No tune

Roll-ing a-long as qui-et as can be,
Rolling a-cross the wide blue sea,
Roll-ing and roll-ing and roll-ing a-long,
Roll-ing a-cross the big wide sea.

Discuss snow in general, especially if the children live in an area where they have little exposure, if any, to snow. What is it made of? How does it feel? What happens if you put a handful in your pocket? Discuss how to make a snowman.

BUILD A LITTLE SNOWMAN
Tune: *I'm a Little Teapot*

Build a lit-tle snow-man,
Start-ing with his feet,
Pile on lots of snow and
Pat it on his feet.
Then you make a round ball,
Put it up on top,
But then the sun will come out
And make the snow-man hot.

Slow

And now he starts to melt
And drip a-way.
He drips and he drips
And he drips all day.
Look-ing for the snow-man,
What do I see?
Noth-ing but a pud-dle,
Where he used to be.

THE BIG SNOWMAN

Tune: *I'm a Little Teapot*

Slowly

First the snow-man's lit-tle
Way down near the ground.
He keeps grow-ing tall-er
Till he's big and round.
Then the sun starts shin-ing,
And be-gins to melt the snow.
Good-bye, lit-tle snow-man,
It's time for you to go.

Now I'm just a pud-dle, float-ing on the ground,
Then I start to roll all a-round and a-round.
And the sun starts shin-ing
And I be-gin to dry.
Oh fare-well lit-tle pud-dle,
Good-bye, good-bye, good-bye.

Slowly

ROCKING BOAT

No tune — soft and quiet

Easiest way

Did you e-ver see a rock-ing boat,
On its back so flat?
Hands hold-ing on-to its knees,
And stay-ing just like that.
Then a-rock and a-rock and a-rock, rock, rock,
All a-cross the sea,
A-rock and a-rock and a-rock, rock, rock,
Rock a-long with me.

Difficult

Did you e-ver see a rock-ing boat,
On its tum-my flat?
Hands in front and feet in back,
And stay-ing just like that.
Then a-rock and a-rock and a-rock, rock, rock,
All a-cross the sea,
A-rock and a-rock and a-rock, rock, rock,
Rock a-long with me.

More difficult

Did you e-ver see a rock-ing boat,
On its tum-my flat?
Hands hold-ing on-to its feet,
And stay-ing just like that.
Then a-rock and a-rock and a-rock, rock, rock,
All a-cross the sea,
A-rock and a-rock and a-rock, rock, rock,
Rock a-long with me.

17 Resting Games

During any one rhythmic activity session, it is usually a good plan to alternate some of the more vigorous activities with one or two quiet games. This gives the child an opportunity to rest without actually "resting." Through these games, sensory-motor growth and perceptual skills are developed. These games require the use of imagination, the need to listen carefully, and the ability to be flexible in changing from one stimulus to another.

Two approaches are used. In the first, the child starts out by resting, listens to clues for movements and dramatization, and then reacts to those clues. In the second, the movements and dramatization come first and are followed by resting.

LITTLE BIRDS
Tambourine
Soft and gentle

All the lit-tle birds are a-sleep in their nest.
All the lit-tle birds are tak-ing a rest.
They do not e-ven twit-ter, they do not e-ven tweet.
Ev'ry-thing is qui-et up and down the street.
Then came the moth-er bird and tapped them on the head,
They o-pened up one lit-tle eye and this is what was said,
"Come lit-tle bir-dies, it's time to learn to fly,
Come lit-tle bir-dies, fly way up to the sky."

Repeat as many times as needed for the activity

Fly, fly, oh, fly a-way, fly, fly, fly,
Fly, fly, oh, fly a-way, fly a-way so high.
Fly, fly, oh, fly a-way, birds can fly the best,
Fly, fly, oh, fly a-way, now fly back to your nest.

The "Octopus Game" gives another experience in close teacher-child involvement. The teacher may find it best to limit the "octopuses" to not more than three or four at a time, unless she is completely prepared to be overwhelmed, at least momentarily.

OCTOPUS GAME
Tambourine

There's a big, black oc-to-pus a-sleep-ing in the sea.
Sh. The oc-to-pus is sleep-ing.
Sh. The oc-to-pus is sleep-ing.
Sh. The oc-to-pus is sleep-ing now.
Yes, a big, black oc-to-pus is sleep-ing in the sea.
He fi-nal-ly wakes up and looks right at me.
He un-wraps his legs and starts out to swim.
So I turn a-round and swim a-way from him.
There's a big, black oc-to-pus swim-ming in the sea,
He fi-nal-ly gets tired try-ing to catch me.
He has so man-y legs that are float-ing in the deep,
He wraps them all a-round him-self and goes to
     sleep.

Kinesthetic awareness can be further reinforced by following up such activities with a discussion of "How did it feel?" Ask the children, "How did it feel inside when you were pretending to be a bird?" Discuss how they made themselves feel like being "octopuses." Ask the children how it feels to be quiet.

Let's find out how it feels to be caterpillars and butterflies.

CATERPILLAR AND BUTTERFLY GAME
Spoken

One day I saw a black, fuzzy caterpillar crawling along. First he'd move the front part of his body, stretching it way out. Then, he'd bring the back part of himself up to meet the front half. He was a very funny stretchy caterpillar.

FUZZY CATERPILLAR
Improvise tune
Tambourine

Oh, Mis-ter cat-er-pil-lar, walk-ing down the street,
Why do you crawl if you have so man-y feet?
With so man-y feet, why can't you run?
Oh, Mister cat-er-pil-lar, crawl-ing in the sun,
Run, run, run, run, run, run, run, run.
Mis-ter fuz-zy cat-er-pil-lar, run, run, run.

Spoken

The caterpillar was so beautiful that I wanted to keep him. I put him in a jar with some little twigs to hold onto. (*The teacher may put the "caterpillars" into imaginary jars.*) Every day I would look to see what had happened. For a long time, nothing happened. But one day I saw the caterpillar spinning a white thread out of his mouth and spinning it all around him. He was holding onto the twig and going 'round and 'round and 'round.

SPINNING MY COCOON
Tune: *Row, Row, Row*

Spin, spin, my co-coon,
Spin it all a-round.
Spin it, wind it, spin it, wind it,
'Round and 'round and 'round.

Spoken

The cocoon slept for many weeks. But one day when I looked into the jar, I saw a beautiful butterfly holding onto one of the twigs. It couldn't fly yet, but it began to move its wings back and forth. I took it outdoors and let it fly away.

FLAP YOUR WINGS
Tambourine
Lilting

Un-fold your wings, lit-tle but-ter-fly,
Look up and see the wide blue sky.
Flap your wings back to and fro,
Flap them a-gain and a-way you go.

59

"Flower Seeds" is a resting game that is important to curriculum reinforcement. It is excellent for improvisation and dramatization, and it may be shortened or extended. This activity is best when the teacher participates and demonstrates some clues as she chants.

For a longer rest period, the seeds may be watered by the farmer; the rain may fall; and the sun can warm the ground before the flowers peek through.

FLOWER SEEDS

Tambourine
Lightly

Note: Instruction for teacher participation precedes each activity.

(The teacher gets down on her knees and makes herself small.)

All the lit-tle flower seeds sleep in the ground.
Warm and snug-gly and tucked in all a-round,
Sleep-ing, oh so sound-ly the long win-ter through,
There real-ly was-n't ver-y much else for them to
    do.
There real-ly was-n't ver-y much else for them to
    do.

(The teacher "peeks" by lifting her head, placing her hands over her eyebrows, and looking all around.)

Now their eyes they o-pened and they peeked
    a-round,

(The teacher "grows" unfolding her arms slowly.)

And start-ed to grow right up through the ground.
They grew so ver-y slow-ly, but they grew straight
    and tall.
And their leaves they un-fold-ed and waved at us
    all.
And their leaves they un-fold-ed and waved at us
    all.

*(The teacher smiles big, while a child, up on a
chair, is the sun.)*

Then the sun shined down and made the flow-ers
    smile,
And they swayed and they swayed in the breeze
    for a-while.
And they swayed and they swayed in the breeze
    for a-while.

*(The teacher plays the part of the wind. A child
may play the part of the wind.)*

Un-til a big wind came and blew them all a-way,
And there were no more flow-ers that day.
And there were no more flow-ers that day.

18 Throwing and Catching

Although some children, especially boys, learn to throw and catch during the pre-school years, it remains a difficult skill for most nursery children to acquire.

Catching a ball is particularly difficult, since it usually moves faster than the child, and it requires skilled visual-motor ability. Catching a balloon is much easier because it is larger and moves slower, giving the child an opportunity to coordinate his movements with the balloon.

A suggested way of developing throwing and catching abilities is to begin with a single balloon. It should be explained to the children before playing balloon games that they are made of rubber and that unless they are handled with care, they may burst and make a loud noise. It is advisable to have several extra balloons on hand in case one "pops." These activities may begin by having the teacher throw the balloon to each child in turn. The child tries to catch it and throw it back to the teacher. Following the teacher-child procedure, have the children throw the balloon to each other. Next, the teacher throws the balloon into the air and the children hit it gently as it floats toward them, trying to keep it in the air. Gradually add more balloons until there is one for every three or four children. To enhance the enjoyment of this activity, a slow waltz may be played on the phonograph; however, it is not expected that the balloon will synchronize its movement with the music. Later, substitute a light weight beach ball for throwing and catching.

Improvise a chant or tune to "I'm a Big Balloon" as the children play the game. Rhythmic accompaniment should not be used since balloons do not make any noise as they float in the air.

I'M A BIG BALLOON

Slow and gentle

I'm a big bal-loo-oo-oon,
A floating, soft bal-loo-oo-oon
A rub-ber-y, round bal-loo-oo-oon,
Floating to the top.

THE LOST BALLOON

Spoken

I was at a circus parade one day. A clown gave me a big, red balloon. I held it up high so everyone could see it. But I accidentally let go of the string and the balloon flew away.

Chant or sing

Oh, fly a-way, fly a-way, my bal-loon,
So far a-way, far a-way, my bal-loon.

Repeat the chant several times, getting softer and softer as the balloon "flies farther away."

These activities may be followed with play utilizing 20"-24" plastic beach balls. Trying to balance on these balls as though swimming is an excellent kinesthetic experience and aids perceptual development.

19 Posture and Balance

Through these body movements, the child learns about postural control and refines his ability to balance and to move with ease. As an infant, he had to learn to balance his head in order to hold it straight up and to balance his torso in order to sit up alone. Later, he had to learn to balance his whole body in order to stand and to walk. Balancing, then, becomes an important aspect of a developmental program for the pre-school child and many activities should be provided to help him grow in body awareness and control.

Suggested classroom activities may include walking on an imaginary line on the floor; walking on a taut string placed on the floor; walking on a narrow board either on the floor or raised slightly off the floor; and walking on a long strip of narrow carpet. At first, let the child walk at his natural gait; then have him walk slowly. A slow walk is more difficult in retaining balance. Also walk sideways, backwards, and to the middle.

Have the children pretend they are "cats" walking on an imaginary fence. They should react spontaneously to the directions given in the poem as the teacher recites it. Repeat the last four lines as many times as needed to let each child complete the activity.

THE CAT ON THE FENCE

Spoken quietly

When ev'ry-one is fast a-sleep,
My cat goes out to play.
He leaps up-on the tall high fence,
And walks a-long the way.

Slowly

First one foot and then the oth-er,
In a long, straight line,
Slow-ly walk-ing, slow-ly stalk-ing,
That big gray cat of mine.

THE HIGH WIRE WALKER

Spoken

I'm a high wire walk-er
Up so ver-y high,
As I step and step a-long,
I can touch the sky.

Slower

I'm way, way up,
On the tight-rope now.
But I can bal-ance my-self,
Be-cause I know how

20 Transitional Activities

A meaningful developmental rhythmic program can be constantly reinforced throughout the school day, just as the program itself reinforces other activities within the curriculum. Such reinforcement is especially suitable when making a transition from one type of classroom activity to another or from one area to another.

During rhythmic activities, it is not recommended that the teacher sing or chant everything to the children. However, rhythmic accompaniment to instructions for playing games, especially for transitional activities, will stimulate a more immediate response and will help to gather a scattered group together as a unit.

Songs and rhythms used for transitional periods should be very limited in number. Familiarity offers security to the child and makes reinforcement more meaningful.

THE INDIAN THROUGH THE FOREST
Improvise tune

Soft-ly on his tip-tip-toes,
The In-di-an through the for-est goes. Sh! Sh! Sh! Sh!
(Repeat.)

TIPTOES
Improvise tune

Sh . . . . . . the ba-by's sound a-sleep.
On our tip-py toes we creep.
Sh . . . .

THE KITTEN AND THE MOUSE
Whispering

The kit-ten and the lit-tle mouse,
Walk so gent-ly through the house.
Sh . . . .

TO MOVE SELF OR TO MOVE THINGS
Tune: *Clap Your Hands*
Make up verses to suit different occasions.

I take my lit-tle chair and put it o-ver there,
I take my lit-tle chair and put it o-ver there,
I take my lit-tle chair and put it o-ver there,
Put it o-ver there.

I take my lit-tle self and sit in the chair,
I take my lit-tle self and sit in the chair,
I take my lit-tle self and sit in the chair,
Sit down in the chair.

21 Place in Space

All movements which give the child an opportunity to explore and to experience the space around him lead to growth in perceptual understanding and self-awareness. It is surprisingly difficult for an adult to realize that although he moves willfully and purposefully, a child is frequently confused with "location" words, especially in relationship to his own self.

The child should be given many opportunities to participate in activities which require him to locate himself in specific places, to understand directionality, and to orient himself to the size and availability of space.

These activities can be reinforced with practice in locating specific objects about the room, or in placing objects in specific places according to directions. Ask a child to place an eraser on top of the desk, to put it under the table, or to place it on the chalkboard. Discuss many things with the children relating to place in space, such as "Which is the front of the table?" and "If you stood on the other side of it, where would the front be?"

Games, with or without props, are excellent for developing a perceptual understanding of place in space. In preparation for "The Bear Went Over the Mountain" game, make obstacle courses with various objects to represent mountains, bridges, trees, and streams to be climbed over, under, or walked around. At the conclusion of the game, ask each "bear" what he saw at the various locations. Children delight in making up new verses to this familiar tune.

THE BEAR WENT OVER THE MOUNTAIN
Tune: same

The bear went o-ver the moun-tain,
The bear went o-ver the moun-tain,
The bear went o-ver the moun-tain,
To see what he could see.

The bear went un-der the big bridge,
The bear went un-der the big bridge,
The bear went un-der the big bridge,
To see what he could see.

In playing "My Bonnie Lies Over the Ocean," divide the children into two groups. One half stands "over the ocean." On appropriate clues, the other half goes "over the ocean," and each child brings back one "bonnie." Although seemingly simple, this is a complicated activity for the young child, and it should be introduced with much patience.

MY BONNIE LIES OVER THE OCEAN

Tune: same

My bon-nie lies o-ver the o-cean,
My bon-nie lies o-ver the sea,
My bon-nie lies o-ver the o-cean,
Oh, bring back my bon-nie to me.
Bring back, bring back,
Bring back my bon-nie to me, to me.
Bring back, bring back,
Oh, bring back my bon-nie to me.

When playing the "Animal Game," decide ahead of time where the farmhouse is; where the cowbarn is; where the henhouse is; and where the other "animals" in the game live. After each child decides which "animal" he will be, he goes to the appropirate area and stays there until it is his turn to respond. When the animal which he is portraying is mentioned, he comes out of his place and acts his part. When he is finished, he returns to his own place. Pictures might be used to indicate the various areas.

ANIMAL GAME
Tune: *Old MacDonald*
Each animal makes its own sound.

Old Mac-Don-ald had a farm,
EE-I-EE-I-OH.
And on this farm he had some ducks,
EE-I-EE-I-OH.
With a quack quack here,
And a quack quack there,
Here a quack, there a quack,
Ev'ry-where a quack quack,
Old Mac-Don-ald had a farm
EE-I-EE-I-OH.

A good game for location, direction, control of speed, and group identity is "Traffic." Discuss in advance where the roadway will be and set up the rules for driving.

TRAFFIC

Rules

All cars must go in the same direction.
All cars must obey the traffic signals.
All drivers must obey the traffic officers.
Speeding is not allowed.
Cars must not bump into other cars.
Cars must not block traffic.

Routine (Vary according to interests of the group.)

Everyone start your cars. Warm up the motor.
Wait for the traffic signal to turn green.
The signal says "GO." The cars move ahead.
The signal says "STOP." Everyone must stop.
Children who do not stop are given a traffic ticket.

The signal says "GO."

You are on the freeway now. You may go a little faster. Now, slow down to get off the freeway.

You have a flat tire. You will have to get out of the car and fix the tire. Be sure to pull off to the right side of the road.

Now, you are downtown. Drive very slowly and watch the traffic signals.

You have just run out of gasoline. You will have to get out of the car and walk to the station. Put the gasoline in the car.

Start the car and drive home very carefully.

22 Descriptive Words

As the child's self-image continues to develop, his sensory and perceptual abilities can be further heightened by relating himself to descriptive words that tell him how to modify a particular movement as he dramatizes a game from cues given by the teacher. Adjectives such as loud, soft, happy, sad, quick, and slow give additional clues to the child for a more refined performance. Adverbs, modifying the adjectives, verbs, or other adverbs, make the directions even more adventuresome.

The following activities are planned for individual participation. Each child takes a turn as the others watch. The child's own name should be substituted for the name given in the text.

DOING WHAT THE MUSIC SAYS
Tune: *Mary Wore a Red Dress*

Bet-ty is walk-ing slow-ly, slow-ly, slow-ly,
Bet-ty is walk-ing slow-ly, all day long.

Jim is leap-ing qui-et-ly, qui-et-ly, qui-et-ly,
Jim is leap-ing qui-et-ly, all day long.

Hap-py Jane is skip-ping, skip-ping, skip-ping,
Hap-py Jane is skip-ping, all day long.

I LOOKED OUT THE WINDOW
Tambourine

I looked out the win-dow and what did I see?
A big black train a-com-ing to-ward me.
I looked out the win-dow and what did I see?
A big black train a-com-ing **to-ward me.**

I looked out the win-dow and what did I see?
A big brown bear a-com-ing to-ward me.
I looked out the win-dow and what did I see?
A big brown bear a-com-ing to-ward me.

I looked out the win-dow and what did I see?
A cute rag-doll a-walk-ing to-ward me.
I looked out the win-dow and what did I see?
A cute rag-doll a-walk-ing to-ward me.

These activities can be followed up with the dramatic interpretation of stories that employ many descriptive words. If the story has action, the teacher may embellish it with additional adverbs and adjectives as she goes on.

23 Spontaneous Movement to Recorded Music

"Free" dancing to recorded music should be introduced after the child has had many experiences in rhythmic movement. However, guidelines should still be employed so that the experience will be meaningful to the child and he will have a place to take off from. These guidelines may be simply casual conversation or they may be stories and poems such as the following. As the child becomes more and more familiar with them, he will, in turn, become increasingly creative.

THE TOY SHOP

Once upon a time, I had a toy shop. At the end of the day, I locked the door and went home. Do you know what happened when I was gone? All the toys woke up. They turned on a record player and began to dance. But as soon as I opened the door the next day, they all stopped dancing. When I turned on the light, all the toys were just sitting around. But I knew what had happened, because the record player was still on. (Play an appropriate record to dramatize.)

RAG DOLL

Let each "rag doll" create his own dance.

If I were a rag doll,
And I be-longed to you,
When-ev-er I would try to dance,
This is what I'd do.

74

THE CIRCUS CLOWN

Did you e-ver see a cir-cus clown
When he goes out to play?
He does-n't play like you and me,
He clowns a-round all day.
He jumps and bends and twists a-round,
And makes a fun-ny face,
He runs and crawls and hoots and toots,
And laughs in ev'ry place.

Let the children dance like circus clowns.

PARADE

I love to watch the big pa-rade
And lis-ten for the band.
And see the peo-ple that have come
From ev'ry dis-tant land.
I see the clowns and el-e-phants
And all the hors-es, too
And all the march-ers on their way
Just like me and you.

DANCING GIRLS

Danc-ing girls are tall and straight,
And smile at ev'ry-one.
They turn and kick and wave their arms
And run and run and run.
They are so love-ly when they dance,
And sway back to and fro,
They stop and throw a kiss at you

Have the children improvise a "free ballet."

And then a-way they go.

24 Hand Movements

As a mother holds her new-born child for the first time, she looks in wonderment at the beauty of his perfectly shaped hand. Likewise, as the father bends down to the new-born child, he marvels at the determination of the baby's grip on his finger.

From birth on, a child's hands set him apart from all other animals. They do his work for him, and they help him to visualize his world. The child's hands reflect his personality and complement his emotions and feelings.

In that part of the brain which controls muscular movements of the body, the largest area is devoted to the hands. The brain records thousands of impressions of how things "feel" to the touch as the hands signal for information. When hand movements are coordinated with eye movements, the resultant perceptual understanding leads to increased intellectual growth.

Since manipulation of the smaller muscles in the hands and fingers requires much greater motor control than the other activities in *Creative Movement for the Developing Child,* mirror techniques are employed. In this procedure, the child imitates the actions of the teacher, but reverses the left or right hand actions, as if he were looking in a mirror.

Finger, hand and arm games not only provide opportunities for added rhythmic movement experiences, but they also help the child to locate various parts of his body, which is essential to the growth and the development of the pre-school child.

A large repertoire is not essential. It is far better to limit the number of games during a school year so that the child becomes sufficiently familiar with them to perform without the aid of the teacher. Finger and hand games are excellent activities for transitional periods. They may be used while waiting for a new activity or while participating in resting games. They may even serve as a calming technique prior to going home.

MAKE A FIST
Adapt to *Little Brown Jug*

Clap my hands and make a fist,
Tap my-self up-on the wrist,
Wig-gle my fin-gers and wig-gle my toes,
Feel the ma-te-ri-al in my clothes.
Point straight up and then point down,
Pull your mouth in-to a frown,
Slap your arm and tap the chair,
Pull ver-y soft-ly on your hair.
Snap your fin-gers if you can,
Then walk a-way like a lit-tle man.

UP AND OVER
Tune: *John Brown's Body*

Two lit-tle hands with which I touch and which
      I feel,
My eye-brows and my el-bows and then way down
      to my heel.
Next up to my cheeks just like I'm go-ing right to
      bed,
Then way up to my head.

Un-der-neath my chin and then on top of my two
      knees,
Shad-ing both my eyes and al-so help-ing me to
      see.
Touch-ing both of my two arms, then touch-ing
      both my feet,
And now I'm touch-ing you.

The side of my hips and then the tip of my toes,
Un-der-neath of both my knees and then down to
    my toes,
I put them down be-side me at the two sides of
    my chair,
Then way high in the air.

Two lit-tle hands with which I touch and which I
    feel,
My eye-brows and my el-bows and then way
    down to my heel,
Then next to each oth-er like I'm get-ting read-y
    to clap,
Then right down on my lap.

DO WHAT I SAY, NOT WHAT I DO
Spoken

Put your hands on top of your head.
    (*Teacher does the same.*)
Put your hands on your knees.
    (*Teacher does the same.*)
Put your hands on your toes.
    (*Teacher does the same.*)
Put your hands on your ears.
    (*Teacher does the same.*)
Put your hands on top of your head.
    (*Teacher puts hands on shoes.*)

In addition to teaching body awareness, "Do What I Say, Not What I Do" is an excellent exercise for auditory perception.

"This Little Boy" is a traditional finger game in which the children pantomime the actions indicated in the poem. The activity may be greatly enhanced by interpolating many other things the "little boy" does in his daily routine, such as putting on his sox and shoes, putting on his shirt and buttoning it, brushing his teeth and washing his face, and so on.

THIS LITTLE BOY

This lit-tle boy is go-ing to bed.
    (*Place the forefinger in the opposite palm.*)
Down on the pil-low he lays his head.
    (*Same action.*)
He cov-ers him-self with the blan-kets so tight.
    (*Fold fingers over the boy.*)
This is the way he sleeps all night.
    (*Place hands to the side of the face, eyes closed.*)
In the morn-ing, he op-ens his eyes.
Back with a toss, the cov-ers they fly.
He jumps out of bed and gets all dressed,
Then off to school to play with the rest.
    (*Fingers run up the arm.*)

25 Body Percussion

During the course of the program, the child has been made constantly aware of his ability to have some control over the gradation of noise that can be made by his body. He has learned that he can walk or run softly or that he can be a dinosaur and stamp loudly. He has learned that "tip-toes" make quiet noise, and that he can even jump making almost no noise at all.

Body percussion games can be introduced to further the child's awareness that he can utilize the various parts of his body to produce deliberate sounds. Name clapping is an excellent exercise in body percussion, and the children delight in discovering how many different rhythms can be applied to their names as they clap their hands while speaking their names. In the following example, vertical lines indicate where the accent may fall.

| | || | | || |
Ma-ry Ben-net   Ma-ry Ben-net

Finger snapping is also a good body percussion source. Some children may find this activity difficult, but they are usually able to do it with practice. Then they may perform this activity to the steady beat or to the rhythmic pattern of the music.

CLICK, CLICK, CLICK
Chant

I take my heel and go click, click, click.
I slap my knees and go smack, smack, smack.
I slide my feet and go shuff, shuff, shuff.
Shuff, shuff, shuff my feet.
I take my tongue and go click, click, click.
I take my lips and go smack, smack, smack.
I take my feet and go stamp, stamp, stamp.
Stamp, stamp, stamp my feet.

26 Percussion Instruments

A natural sequence in the development of a rhythmic movement program is the introduction of percussion instruments to the child. Percussion instruments fall into two classifications. They are either pitched or non-pitched. Only the non-pitched instruments will be considered here since *Creative Movement for the Developing Child* is concerned primarily with rhythm.

The technique which a child acquires in learning to use a wide assortment of percussion instruments not only tends to improve his tactile versatility, but also increases his perceptual-motor skills. Although certain "home-made" instruments can serve quite satisfactorily in many rhythmic activities, the necessity of providing some professionally manufactured instruments of good quality cannot be overemphasized. Through their use, the child may obtain full value from percussion experiences. It is highly important that children be taught the proper care of instruments. If they are presented in an orderly, attractive manner, the child will understand that they must be handled carefully. Some of the instruments should be displayed where a child may select them for experimentation during the free play periods.

The use of instruments presents new experiences for the child; therefore, he must first learn to identify them and then be given sufficient time to learn how to play them. This may require some time and much patience, but random beating on a drum is of absolutely no consequence in the learning process.

Percussion instruments have very definite functions, and before they can be used effectively in an elaboration of creative movement, the ability to perform well is essential. The best procedure is to begin with rhythm sticks as they require little coordination between the two hands. After the teacher has demonstrated various ways in which the sticks may be played, the child is given a pair so that he may experiment with them. Can he make them walk, run, hop or gallop? Can they sound like raindrops, clocks ticking, trains running, or a lady typing?

Some teachers prefer to introduce rhythm sticks by using rolled up sheets of newspaper. These prevent the necessity of listening to the weak beats while the child is making his first attempt in tapping out the strong beats.

Gradually add other instruments, preferably wooden ones at first, such as tone blocks, maracas, claves and guiros. Then add certain drums, such as tom-toms and bongos. The children should observe that some of the instruments are shaken; some are struck with a mallet; and some are played with the fingertips or the hand.

As more instruments are added, they may be combined in ensembles to accompany a song or a game. Part of the fun which children derive from experimenting with these instruments is in making decisions as to which ones best mark the beat; the accent; or the rhythmic pattern. Can an instrument help to establish the tempo of a song? Should the intensity of sound be light or heavy? Is a particular musical instrument "right" for a chosen musical selection.

The "Percussion Walk" is excellent in helping children understand which instrument is best suited to a particular movement or sound. Tell a story about taking a walk. As you mention a certain sound, the child who is holding the instrument with which to imitate that sound takes his turn, accompanying the rhythm of the words. The sounds should be decided upon before playing the game. Let the children choose the instruments; however, they may need some help from the teacher if they decide on an instrument which is not appropriate for a certain sound. If desired, the teacher may make a list on the chalkboard of the pre-selected instruments chosen by the children.

PERCUSSION WALK

One day I went for a walk. As I walked along on the sidewalk, I could hear my footsteps going WALK, WALK, WALK. Some other people came by. . . . Their footsteps went WALK, WALK, WALK. . . . I passed a new house. . . . Some men were fixing the roof. I could hear their hammers going TAP, TAP, TAP. . . . I heard a train coming, so I went down to the corner to watch it. My feet went RUN, RUN, RUN. . . . Oh, it was a long train. The wheels going 'round and 'round went CLICK-CLICK-CLACK. . . . Then I saw a man riding in a wagon which was being pulled by a horse. The horse's hoofs went CLIP-CLOP, CLIP-CLOP. . . . It was getting very late. My watch said TICK, TICK, TICK. . . . It was very late for my dinner. I ran all the way home. My feet went RUN, RUN, RUN. . . . I came to my house and knocked on the door. . . . KNOCK, KNOCK, KNOCK. . . . My mother came to the door. I washed my hands and sat down to eat. Everyone was talking. It sounded like a broken television . . . NOISE. (*All instruments.*)

ARE YOU SLEEPING

Tune: *Are You Sleeping?*

Are you sleep-ing, are you sleep-ing?
    (*Wooden instruments*)
Broth-er John, broth-er John.
    (*Add drums and tambourine*)
Morn-ing bells are ring-ing,
    (*Add bells*)
Morn-ing bells are ring-ing,
Ding, ding, dong.
    (*Only triangle plays*)
Ding, ding, dong.

PERCUSSION PLAYER

Tune: *Clap Your Hands*

I take my lit-tle sticks and go tap, tap, tap.
I take my lit-tle sticks and go tap, tap, tap.
I take my lit-tle sticks and go tap, tap, tap.
Tap, tap, tap my sticks.

I take my lit-tle drums and go bong, bong, bong.
I take my lit-tle drums and go bong, bong, bong.
I take my lit-tle drums and go bong, bong, bong.
Bong, bong, bong my drums.

I take my ma-ra-ca and go shake, shake, shake.
I take my ma-ra-ca and go shake, shake, shake.
I take my ma-ra-ca and shake, shake, shake.
Shake, shake, shake my ma-ra-ca.

Substitute other instruments.

In using percussion instruments to accompany a record, explain to the class that they should try to make the music sound better. Tell the children not to play too loud or too hard. It is best to start out with two or three records the children know; then introduce additional records that are especially suitable for a percussion ensemble.

27 Auditory Perception Games

After the child has learned to identify the percussion instruments by sight and has acquired some skill in playing them, more advanced experimentation can further increase auditory-perceptual abilities.

It is relatively easy to identify an instrument if the child is watching it being played. But it is far more difficult to recognize it if it is only heard and not seen. The sound of rhythm sticks made from hollow bamboo can easily be mistaken for temple blocks. A tambourine or a drum produces quite a different sound if it is tapped near the rim rather than on the center of the head.

Auditory perception games can be played to give experiences to the child in "listening without seeing." If the child closes his eyes during these activities, he can devote full attention to the sound.

A specific advantage of auditory perception games is that they help the teacher in ascertaining whether a child is simply "hearing" or actually "listening." If a child is not able to identify a simple rhythmic instrument by its sound, it may very well be the reason that he is not responding with ease to organized movement. Although there are certain correlations between sight and sound, music is entirely dependent on some form of aural perception. It is a highly complex art, the basic components of which are tone and time. Appreciation of the tonal element can be understood only if the rhythmic element of timing is clearly defined in such a way that music becomes as meaningful as language. Rhythm makes music "move" and as the child develops skills in movement, his aesthetic experiences are greatly enhanced.

Suggestions for auditory perception games follow. As the child becomes skilled in these activities, he will derive great enjoyment from the challenge of increasingly more difficult variants.

EYES CLOSED

Each child is asked to close his eyes. When all eyes are closed, the teacher makes several sounds on an instrument. The children are then asked to open their eyes and select the instrument which they thought was being played. This procedure may be varied by having a child be the "teacher."

PLAYING "IT"

One child sits in a chair with his back to the group. Each child in the class is given a different instrument. The teacher selects one child to play his instrument. The child who is "It" tries to guess who it was that played. Vary this by having four children with the same kind of instrument take places in different parts of the room. The child who is "It" comes to the center of the room and closes his eyes. One of the four children is directed by the teacher to play his instrument, and the child who is "It" tries to guess where the sound came from.

FIND ME

Several instruments of similar but slightly different sounds are placed on a table. The child is given a duplicate of one of the instruments on the table and is asked to select the one on the table that makes more nearly the sound of the one he has.

COPY CAT

The teacher taps out a simple rhythmic pattern on the tambourine. In echo response, the child tries to duplicate the pattern by clapping his hands or tapping lightly on the table top. Then he tries to duplicate the same pattern with his instrument. In more advanced classes, the children may be chosen to be the "teacher."

Bibliography

ANDREWS, GLADYS. *Creative Rhythmic Movement for Children*. Englewood Cliffs, N.J.: Prentice-Hall, Inc., 1954.

ARNHEIM, RUDOLPH. *Art and Visual Perception*. Berkeley & Los Angeles: University of California Press, 1966.

BUTTOLPH, EDNA G. *Music Without Piano*. New York: Early Childhood Education Council of New York, 1966.

DELECATO, CARL H. *The Diagnosis and Treatment of Speech and Reading Problems*. Springfield, Ill.: Charles C. Thomas, 1963.

GETMAN, G. N. *How To Develop Your Child's Intelligence*. Laverne, Minn.: G. N. Getman, 1962.

HATCHER, CARO C., and MULLIN, HILDA. *More Than Words: Movement Activities for Children*. Pasadena, Calif.: Parents-for-Movement, 1967.

HUNT, J. McV. *Intelligence and Experience*. New York: The Ronald Press, 1961.

KEPHART, NEWELL C. *The Slow Learner in the Classroom*. Columbus, Ohio: Charles E. Merrill Books, Inc., 1960.

KOFFKA, K. *The Growth of the Mind*. Totowa, N.J.: Littlefield, Adams & Company, 1959.

PIAGET, JEAN. *The Origins of Intelligence in Children*. New York: International Universities Press, 1952.

PIAGET, J., and INHELDER, B. *The Child's Conception of Space*. London: Routledge and Kegan Paul, 1956.